MADULO
&
Co.

Other titles in the Hodder African Readers series

The Fearless Four	978 0340 940426
The Fearless Four: Hijack!	978 0340 940419
The Fearless Four and the Graveyard Ghost	978 0340 940358
The Fearless Four and the Smugglers	978 0340 940334
Dead Men's Bones	978 0340 940365
Twin Trouble	978 0340 940310
Sauna and the Drug Pedlars	978 0340 940402
The Power of Corruption	978 0340 940341
Magic, Mystery and Mister Prince	978 0340 940389
Time Bomb	978 0340 940327
God's Case: No Appeal	978 0340 940372
One Man, Two Votes	978 0340 940396
Dear Miss Winfrey	978 0340 984178
Shoot for the Moon	978 0340 984215
The Button Bottle	978 0340 984222
The Mystery of Rukodzi Mountain	978 0340 984239
A Few Little Lies	978 0340 984154
Conquest & Conviviality	978 0340 984161
Secret Celebrity	978 0340 984208
No More Secrets	978 0340 984192

Madulo & Co.

By Dabilo M. Mokobi

Illustrated by Joseph Mugisha

AN HACHETTE UK COMPANY

Orders: please contact Hachette UK Distribution, Hely Hutchinson Centre, Milton Road, Didcot, Oxfordshire, OX11 7HH. Telephone: +44 (0)1235 827827. Email: education@hachette.co.uk. Lines are open from 9 a.m. to 5 p.m., Monday to Friday. You can also order through our website: www.hoddereducation.com

© Dabilo M. Mokobi 2008
First published in this edition in 2008 by Hodder Education,
An Hachette UK Company
Carmelite House
50 Victoria Embankment
London EC4Y 0DZ

The authorised representative in the EEA is Hachette Ireland, 8 Castlecourt Centre, Dublin 15, D15 XTP3, Ireland (email: info@hbgi.ie)

Impression number 10 9 8 7 6
Year   2025

All rights reserved. Apart from any use permitted under UK copyright law, no part of this publication may be reproduced or transmitted in any form or by any means, electronic or mechanical, including photocopying and recording, or held within any information storage and retrieval system, without permission in writing from the publisher or under licence from the Copyright Licensing Agency Limited. Further details of such licences (for reprographic reproduction) may be obtained from the Copyright Licensing Agency Limited, www.cla.co.uk

Cover and illustration by Joseph Mugisha
Typeset in 12/14 Bembo by Manoj Sookai
Printed and bound in Great Britain by Clays Ltd, Elcograf S.p.A.
A catalogue record for this title is available from the British Library

ISBN: 978 0340 98 418 5

Chapter One

'I can't stand it!' cried Madulo. Her head was stuck under a pillow and one fist was raised up in the air. 'I can't stand it any more! I can't sleep! I just *can't sleep!*'

She had huge butterflies in her stomach and felt as if she could run around the block three times. It was almost morning and Madulo had been tossing and turning since she'd woken at midnight. The reason for Madulo's nervous state? A week in Serowe without her mum, without her best friend, *without* TV and, worst of all, a bus-ride to Serowe – on her own! Sometimes she felt that 12 years old was quite mature. Right now, she felt that 12 years old was way too young to travel about the country on her own. Going on a long trip alone for the first time, this was exciting – but terrifying too.

Another part of her wanted to get out of Gaborone. She had telephoned her cousin Lema

last night and they were all looking forward to her arriving . . . today. This was it. The sun was creeping out of the sky and the day was about to begin. There was no point trying to sleep any more either. That would be wasted sleep because she would have to wake up again in . . . well, in a very short while.

Madulo rolled from one side of her three-quarter bed to the other. This was the last time she would be alone in a bed for three weeks. In Serowe beds are shared. Everybody is packed together like sardines. And there are no sheets in the beds in Serowe. Just thick scratchy blankets that make you itch in winter, or a thin brightly coloured bedspread in summer. Thank God it was summer. There would be no scratchy blankets this time.

'Hey, I'm going to have to get used to eating lunch late too,' Madulo thought, 'and no bacon and sausages for breakfast. And going to collect all that heavy water from the standpipes in buckets . . . m-m-m-m-m, just lovely!' Then she remembered something else – something she had been trying to forget about: '. . . and going to the PIT LATRINE!' She screamed, with her head still under her pillow, so as not to frighten her mother.

'Oh no! The pit latrine . . . YUCK! And all those lizards in there . . . Double-Yuck! When I grow older, I'm going to build Nkuku a proper toilet, like the one we have here. One that is in the house! Eeeeish!' Slowly, Madulo breathed out. It wasn't going to help. She was going, pit-latrine or no pit-latrine, so she might as well just get on with it.

Madulo lay flat and very still and closed her eyes. She thought about all the weird things she loved and hated about Serowe. Especially the adventures she and her cousin got up to. She really looked forward to seeing Lema and everyone again . . . really, she did.

'Madulo! Mad-uuuuu-looo! Are you awake, my child?' her mother called.

Madulo sat bolt upright and jumped out of bed. She must have fallen asleep again after all. How did that happen? *When* did that happen? What time *was* it now?

'Ye-e-e-s, Mama. I'm up. Is it time to go?

Have I missed the bus?' Madulo quickly tried to get dressed, while throwing a handful of her most precious things in her small rucksack at the same time.

Her mother appeared at the bedroom door. She laughed when she saw the state Madulo was in. 'Madulo, the bus leaves at one o'clock this afternoon. It's half past eight in the morning. You have plenty of time to get ready!'

'Whew!' sighed Madulo, 'OK Mama, I'll start packing just now.'

★★★

The morning seemed to take forever. And what should she pack? Should she take her short skirt? (No, Nkuku wouldn't like that!) Should she take her new takkies? (No, they might get dirty.) Should she take her stuffed toy dog? (No, the others might laugh at her for being a baby.) But at last it was time to go – and she was able to close her suitcase, with a bit of help from Mama.

On the way to the bus station, Madulo couldn't sit still. 'And Mama, what if I fall asleep on the bus and the horrible bus driver doesn't stop when he's supposed to, and I end up somewhere far and dangerous, and you never see me again?' Nervously, Madulo opened the window then shut it again. She fiddled with the radio station and the volume; switched the fan off and then on again.

'Madulo, I'd like to have a radio that works after I drop you off. Will you sit still – and leave those buttons alone!' Mama was a bit nervous too, Madulo thought. 'And how do you know the bus driver is horrible? You can't possibly know that in advance. Just stay *awake* Madulo and get off when you're supposed to. Nkuku will be there to meet you.'

Madulo's mother *was* worried about putting her precious little girl in a bus on her own. But she didn't want Madulo to know that, so she left it at that.

There were many buses parked at the station, most of them old and rusty. Madulo was wondering which one she would be going on, when her mother suddenly stopped in front of the oldest and rustiest looking one.

'Mama! This bus will never make it to Serowe!' Madulo cried in horror. 'Look at it Mama!'

'Madulo, this is Bra-Peter's bus company. He's the only bus owner I can entrust you to. His buses may be old but they work. Now jump in and take a seat. You'll be fine honey. Don't lose your rucksack.'

A short plump man climbed into the driver's seat and looked in the mirror above his head. Madulo looked into his eyes in the mirror and gave him the sweetest smile she could manage. The bus driver just made a sour face and blew his rather large nose on a dirty handkerchief.

'I knew it!' thought Madulo. 'He's horrible!'

The bus roared to a start and jugga-jugga-jugged slowly out of the station. When the driver made a turn, the people standing up had to hang on to the overhead rails to keep their balance.

Madulo's mother stood on the pavement and watched as the old bus pulled off. As she was waving to her little girl, she said a short prayer: 'Dear Lord, there are many things that I ask of you. Please forget all of them and do only this: take care of my little girl. Make sure she gets home safe. Amen.'

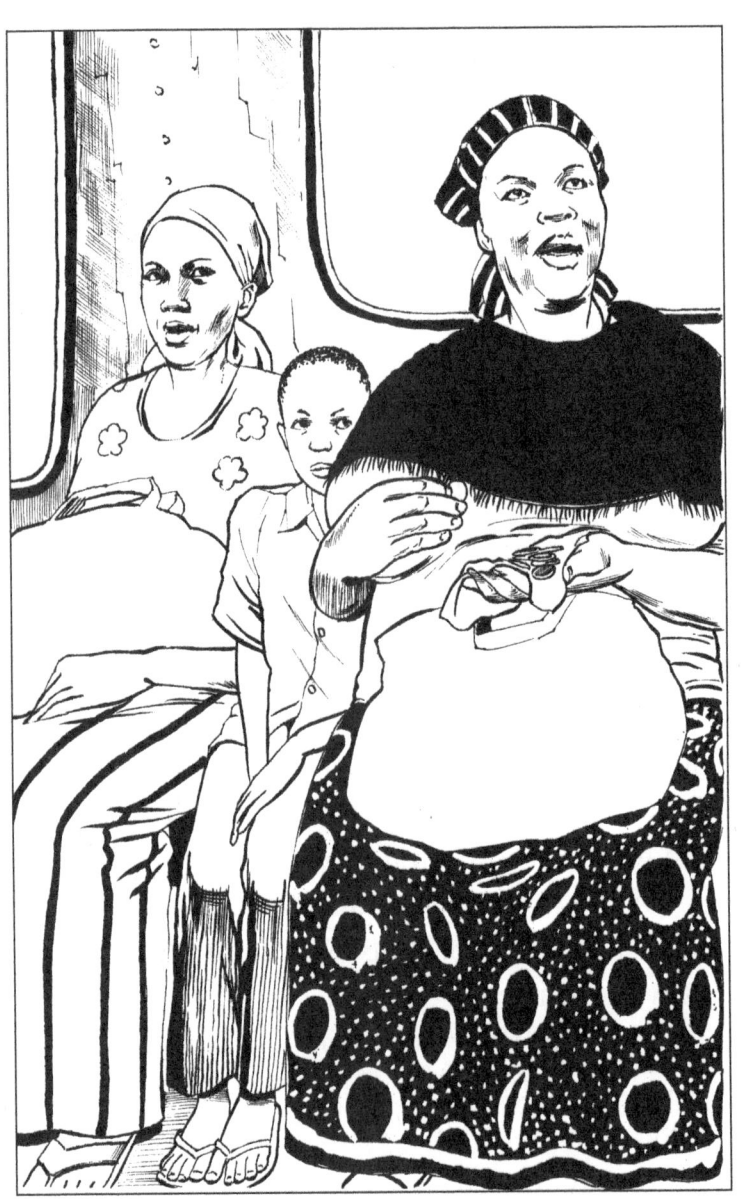

As they moved out of Gaborone, towards Mochudi, the bus conductor got up to collect money from all the passengers. Madulo's mother had already paid, so all she had to do was show him the receipt her mother had given her.

When the conductor got to the back of the bus, he found a suspicious-looking teenage boy sitting tightly scrunched up next to two older ladies. One of the ladies was quite enormous and her chest covered part of the boy's face.

'Where are you going Mma?' the conductor asked the smaller lady.

'Palapye, Rra,' she replied in a big booming voice.

'Thirty Pula,' said the conductor.

She pulled a handkerchief out of her blouse, unrolled it carefully and paid the man with the correct number of five-Pula coins.

'And you, Mma?' he said in an unfriendly voice to the enormous lady.

'Palapye too, Rra!' she replied in a rather small and gentle voice. 'We're sisters travelling together.'

'Ee, thirty Pula,' said the man. 'You obviously eat all the food,' he mumbled rudely.

She shuffled and shifted, and nearly squashed the sandwiched boy, before finally paying her dues.

'And the boy?' huffed the conductor.

The two ladies looked at the boy and shrugged their shoulders.

'Hey you!' sneered the conductor. 'Where are you going? It's time to pay.'

The boy ducked deeper behind the enormous lady and looked up at the ceiling. He was a thin, clever-looking boy, about Madulo's age. He caught her looking at him and gave a little half-smile – so quickly that Madulo wondered if she had imagined it. Then he was looking back out of the window again.

He kept his hands on his lap. Still he said nothing.

Suddenly the conductor woke up to what was going on. 'Boy!' he shouted. 'Stop fooling around. Pay now or get off!'

The boy shifted about but he didn't even look at the conductor. The bus trundled on its way, while the passengers looked on, interested to see something happening on the long, boring journey.

'Hee-ee-ey, Moreti!' shouted the conductor to the driver. 'Stop the bus . . . stop now! This boy is trying to cheat us. Wena!' He pointed at the boy. 'Get up! Quickly!'

Then he took a deep breath, seeming to take in all the air on the bus and then bellowed at the boy: 'GET OFF THE BUS! NOW!'

The bus came to a sharp stop and Madulo nearly bashed her head against the seat in front of her. The teenage boy squeezed out from between the two ladies and snaked through the standing passengers. The conductor poked and pinched him all the way off the bus.

'Iyoooo! Ooucchh! Iyoooo! Ooucch!' he cried.

As he jumped off the bus he shouted: 'THIS IS MY STOP ANYWAY!' and ran off into the bush. Everybody on the bus looked back to see what would happen next. Once he was sure that the bus was moving, he appeared again and started dancing and waving his hands about, and sticking out his tongue at the conductor.

'Crazy village boy!' huffed the bus driver. 'His father obviously didn't punish him enough when he was younger!'

Madulo smiled. She wished she could have spoken to the cheeky boy who didn't pay. He looked fun. She looked out again at the view from the window. Botswana was beautiful. But there wasn't much happening out there. Just a few goats standing in the shade of a thorn tree and – sometimes – a donkey cart going past.

She settled back into her seat for the rest of the journey, looking forward to telling Lema about the trouble on the bus. She sat quietly and prayed that she wouldn't miss her stop. That would cost more than her mother had paid for. More importantly, she hoped that Nkuku and Lema would be waiting for her when she got off.

Chapter Two

Madulo's heels rested steadily against the big Marula tree in the front of the yard. She was trying to break the record for the world's longest handstand. She squinted against the sun, and spoke to her cousin's socks. She had obviously been thinking about something while she was upside-down. 'Lema, we can't go exploring alone,' she said, 'it might be dangerous.'

'OK, we can ask Noah and Letso if they want to come along. But you know those boys . . . they always want something for themselves before they do anything for anyone. What will we give them?'

'Well, luckily, I brought my old radio with me. It works with batteries. I have a new one at home so I can give them this one. They'll like it, I'm sure,' Madulo offered generously (still upside down).

'Thoooo!' She dropped her feet to the ground.

'Come on then Lema.'

The boys loved the idea of swapping their company on an expedition for a radio. They immediately jumped up, ready to set off – but it wasn't as easy as all that.

It had taken hours just to organise a simple expedition, Madulo thought crossly. It would have been much faster in the city. First the boys had to finish their work around the house and Madulo and Lema had to make sure all the water-buckets were full, and Lema's mother had asked her to run to the shop and get sugar. Were they ever going to get anywhere? The afternoon rain clouds were beginning to pile up in the high sky. The best of the day was nearly over!

Madulo had heard many stories about the strange things that happened at her home village. When Nkuku visited them in the city, she would always bring a tale about an old woman who was accused of being a witch, or a little boy who was swallowed by a BIG snake that lives in the

Newtown River, or the girl who lost her voice after saying rude things to her mother.

Although Madulo did not believe half of the stories, she was curious. She wanted to meet the old witch. She also wanted to see the big river snake for herself. But Madulo knew that children were not allowed to go anywhere alone, especially not in Serowe. She knew that – but she still wanted to go.

'Hey, where are we going?' shouted Madulo to the boys when they finally got going that afternoon.

'Just keep up with us !' Noah shouted over his shoulder.

The four of them ran across the village fields, jumping over ditches and slapping tree leaves that hung low enough for their reach.

As they fell about playfully, Madulo noticed a packet of something sticking out of Letso's pocket.

'What's that in your pocket, Letso?'

'Oh these? These are some nails from my father's toolbox,' replied Letso smugly.

'What do you need nails for?' Lema asked curiously.

'To make traps with. The other day we met these horrible men and they chased us on their bicycles and took our ball and crushed it. We hadn't done a thing! But we will now! We're going to puncture their tyres,' he laughed to himself at the thought. Noah chuckled in agreement.

Madulo wasn't very sure about this part of the exploring plan, but the girls stood aside as the boys planted nails across the sandy dirt road.

'This will do it,' Letso grinned. 'Let's wait for them behind those bushes.'

After waiting for what seemed like ten hours (although it was actually only 30 minutes), they got tired of hanging around and decided to move on. But they left the nails in the road, just in case.

When they got to the Newtown River it was dry and there were no snakes around. They used old cardboard boxes to slide down rocks and into the dry riverbed. The river sand provided a soft landing. Madulo had never done anything like this. This was better than the hot metal slide she played on at her school.

Then she found a big tree with a strong branch to swing from and dive into the riverbed.

'Be careful Madulo!' Noah shouted. 'There are rocks in there. You might land on one and . . .'

But he spoke too late. And Madulo had chosen the wrong spot. As soon as she hit the ground, she knew she had made a big . . . BIG mistake.

'Aa-a-a-a-h! Ou-u-u-u-ch!' cried Madulo.

Then she went very quiet as the full impact of the pain hit her.

They all gathered around to inspect her bruised knees and hands, and her grazed chin. The worst was her twisted wrist . . . that hurt a lot.

'That stupid, stupid rock! Eeeeish! I thought there was soft sand everywhere . . . ouch!' She tried very hard not to cry. 'How am I going to do handstands now?' she moaned.

'Ao, Madulo,' said Letso feeling sorry for his friend, 'those bruises will be gone by tomorrow. You'll see. We'll be out here again soon. And next time, you'd better be more careful.'

Lema tied Madulo's wrist tightly with the scarf she had been wearing on her head and they set off home. Nobody said much. The grand expedition had not turned out as well as they had hoped! Lema put her arm around her little cousin's shoulder. Madulo kicked a pile of sand. It wasn't *fair*!

★★★

When they came to cross the big dirt road, Letso noticed that the sand had been pushed away where they'd planted the nails earlier.

'Look!' he exclaimed, 'someone's been here. I hope it was those awful men,' he said smugly.

Madulo felt . . . well, she didn't feel very safe, suddenly. First the accident with the rock . . . and now this! She looked around anxiously. But she didn't have much time to think. Just then, two large men jumped out from behind a bush and grabbed them before they had a chance to do anything at all!

'Got you!' shouted the first man, 'I knew we would catch you.'

In one big movement, he grabbed Letso and Madulo's arms and tied them together. Madulo cried out at the pain from her hurt wrist, but the

men didn't care. The second man caught Lema and Noah and tied them together too. Madulo, Letso, Lema and Noah didn't have time to think about what had just happened, or where the men had come from. None of them had time to even *think* about running away.

'B-b-b-b-but we didn't do anything,' stuttered Letso, not looking so smug any more.

'Look Manny, I'm sure this lot planted those nails here,' said the second man, 'and because of them, we missed the train. Hey! Aren't those the boys who were bothering us with their stupid football the other day?'

'You're right Manny,' replied the first man, 'those *are* the same boys! And now they've got friends to help them get in our way. I say we take them back with us. The Boss might believe us if we have them there.'

Madulo and the others were confused. Both men were called Manny. How could that be? Maybe it was a secret code name or something. The two Mannys walked in front of the children and pulled the ropes. As much as the children tried to untie themselves, they couldn't.

A rusty old truck was parked at the bottom of a ditch behind a big Mopane tree. Madulo and the others were loaded in the back and Manny One revved the engine into gear. Manny Two sat in the back and ordered the children to lie face down and not to look up. This was turning out to be one scary adventure.

The journey was long and rough and by the time it ended, all four children were sore everywhere. As soon as they got off the truck, they were blindfolded and led inside a large warehouse. The warehouse was filled with big cardboard boxes with different coloured labels on them. They were steered into a storeroom. They heard a door close and a key turning in the lock.

For a while, nobody said anything. Nobody had anything they really wanted to say. Then Letso whispered into the horrible, quiet, dark, 'Noah! I think I've got my rope a bit loose. Can you get over to me?'

The girls heard the sound of Noah shuffling about and then, after a few minutes, a little squeak of triumph. 'Got it!' A few minutes after that, all four children were free and rubbing their wrists and pulling off the blindfolds.

'Are you OK?' Lema asked Madulo quietly.

'Yes . . . I think I'm OK,' she whispered back. 'Thanks.'

They were in a storeroom – quite a big storeroom, and it was dark, smelly and dusty.

'Letso! What have you got us into?' cried Madulo as she tried to see properly again. There wasn't much light.

'I didn't know *this* would happen,' replied Letso in a small voice. He was *really* scared now.

'He-l-p! He-l-p, u-s!' shouted Lema.

'No one can hear you Lema. We don't even know where we are,' said Noah, who had been very quiet the whole time.

And then . . . they heard footsteps outside the door, and voices.

'Boss, I'm telling you. It's because of those children that we missed the train.'

'Sshh! Listen,' whispered Noah.

'Are you two *crazy*?' bellowed another man, 'Are you telling me that you failed to bring my computers because of a bunch of *children*?'

He sounded very, very angry.

'B-b-b-b-o-s-s . . .' stuttered one of the Mannys, 'it wasn't our fault!'

'Do you *know* how much money you've just lost me?' hissed the man known as the Boss.

'B-b-b-but Boss, we still have some computers here. We can sell these ones . . . see?' The other Manny spoke almost too quietly for his boss to hear.

'And we brought the children with us, so you could see it was true.'

This time the man exploded with anger.

'You did *what*? You *brought* the children! You're much, *much* more stupid than I thought. Completely *stupid*!' barked the Boss.

Lema had heard enough. She remembered the story on the television news about secondary schools around Serowe that were missing brand new computers. The Education Ministry in Gaborone had sent the computers by train in big shipments. But most of the shipments had failed to arrive. The two Mannys and their boss must be the ones who were stealing them.

'Letso, you've got us into some *serious* trouble,' whispered Lema, 'those men are the thieves that have been on the news headlines. And now we know their secret. They could kill us!'

'Come *on* Lema,' Noah hissed back, 'no one is going to *kill* us!'

'They are! They are! They probably kill people all the time!' Lema was shaking with fear.

'Stop it Lema, you're scaring Madulo,' Letso said. 'No one is going to die.'

'How are we going to get out of here?' asked Madulo.

'We'll be in body bags. Dead. And ready to be thrown to wild animals for their supper,' Lema moaned.

'No! Lema, don't say that!' cried Madulo, forgetting to whisper.

BANG, BANG, BANG! Someone thumped on the door.

'Hey you! Be quiet in there!'

★★★

The computers stacked in the warehouse and in the storeroom were all stolen. And there were stolen televisions and radios too. The children saw that from the labels on the boxes. The man the Mannys called 'Boss' was the leader of a gang operating in central Botswana. The Boss ordered the Mannys and other teams of men to steal electronic goods for him to sell. He sold them for less than they were worth . . . but he still made a lot of money.

However things didn't always work out the way the Boss wanted. Today the Mannys were supposed to meet the goods train and collect ten computers from the Station Master, who also worked for the Boss. When they were sent on a mission like that, they used bicycles to get to the train station, to make sure that everything they wanted was off-loaded properly. The Boss had given strict instructions that nothing was to be taken off the train unless the two Mannys were there.

Then the Station Master would drive the two Mannys, their bicycles and the stolen goods back to their own truck, which was parked somewhere in the woods. This was the usual plan. But this plan had not worked today. After what had happened to their bicycles, they had known they wouldn't make it on time. The Station Master could not hold the train for too long. The platform attendant blew his whistle, and the train chugged on towards the next village.

Now the two Mannys worried about what their boss was going to do to them. Maybe he would order some of the other guys to beat them up? Or worse! Or maybe they would be sacked, never to work for the Boss again! Or . . . there was a very scary story around the gang about how the Boss had cut off one of his worker's little fingers for failing to follow orders.

The two Mannys started sweating.

'What are we going to do about those children?' asked Manny Two.

'Well, I'm waiting to find out what the Boss will do to *us* first,' replied Manny One.

'Whatever it is, those kids will pay for it.'

Chapter Three

'Did you hear that Letso?' whispered Madulo, shaking with fear. 'They are going to make us pay for whatever happens to them. We *have* to get out of here!'

Noah paced the room, looking for a way out – or at least something they could use to help them get out. But there was nothing. The only thing that gave him hope was a small square of dim light above his head that looked like a painted-over window. He quietly said a prayer.

'Hey, look, I think that's a window up there,' he said to the others.

Lema jumped up. 'Where?'

'*If* that is a window, Noah, how are you going to open it from here?' asked Letso, quite upset that he hadn't spotted it first.

'Be quiet Letso!' said Madulo angrily. 'You're the one who got us into all this and now you're not helping.' Then she thought for a moment.

'Maybe we could form a human pyramid? Like they do sometimes in films!'

'Nah,' Letso said. 'Have you ever tried to do that? We did, once, at school, and we all fell in a great heap.'

It was Lema who kept her head when everybody else was getting excited and cross. 'I think Noah is right. That *is* a small window up there that's been painted over, that's why there isn't much light coming in. If we pile the boxes up to make steps, we should be able to get up there.'

'All in all,' thought Madulo, as she helped the others with the boxes, 'this was a much better plan.'

It was hot – and heavy – work, but they got the boxes piled to make steps of a sort and Noah was able to wedge himself next to the window and give it a huge push. It gave slightly the first time and then, with one more strong push, it flew open.

Noah used both hands to pull himself up and stuck his head out. He blinked to get his eyes used to the sunlight again. It was a very small window, but he should *just* be able to squeeze through. He saw that luckily they were at the back of the property, where the two Mannys and their boss probably wouldn't see them.

But – and it was a big but – they were still quite high off the ground; too far to jump, especially for Madulo with her hurt knees and wrist.

'I think . . . I think . . .' he puffed, quite out of breath '. . . I've got a plan.'

He dropped back down beside the others to explain.

'It all depends on Madulo. But I'm sure she can do it.' (Madulo felt quite proud when he said that.)

'She is going to have to pretend that she is in terrible pain and needs help.' (That wasn't going to be too difficult, Madulo thought. She hurt just about everywhere!)

'I'll get myself down from the roof . . . somehow . . . and I can see a long hosepipe on a tap on the other side of the yard. If you can get the Mannys in here, and the door open, I'll fling the hosepipe over them and we can all jump them!'

It wasn't very *much* of a plan. But it was the best anybody could think of.

Madulo and the others watched as Noah climbed back up the boxes and his dangling feet disappeared out of the window. After a short pause, they heard a dull thud as he landed on the ground and a grunt of surprise as he found out how far down it really was.

'That was brave!' Lema whispered. 'Now it's your turn, Madulo.'

Madulo arranged herself on a box beside the locked door. For a moment she closed her eyes. She imagined that she was in the school play – on the stage at school. It was her big moment. She was the star.

'Ow-oooooooooooooooooo!'

'Ow-oooooooooooooooooo!'

'OW-OOOOOOOOOOOOOOO!'

Even the other children – who knew she was going to do it – felt the hairs rise on the back of their necks. Outside, there was no sound of the Mannys.

'Ow-oooooooooooooooooo!'

'Ow-oooooooooooooooooo!'

'OW-OOOOOOOOOOOOOOO!'

After another moment of silence, one of the Mannys spoke – in a very worried voice. 'What is it? What's going on in there?'

Madulo gave it another great shot.

'Ow-ooooooooooooooooooo!'
'Ow-ooooooooooooooooooo!'
'OW-OOOOOOOOOOOOOOO!'

There was a shuffling and a muttering . . . and then the sound of the key turning in the lock . . . and the door opening. Light flooded into the storeroom.

And then everything seemed to happen at once! The Mannys stepped in – not really able to see much. Noah quickly got behind them with a huge pile of hosepipe coiled in his arms. He lifted it high and threw it over the Mannys, who struggled and wriggled . . . but couldn't get free. While they were still struggling, the children pushed past them, threw the coils of the hose out of the way, and slammed the door behind them. The Mannys were trapped! Noah locked the door and put the key in his pocket.

'Hang on a minute,' he said, dashing over to

the old truck. 'We might as well make things difficult for them if they do manage to get out.' He reached in through the open window, released the bonnet catch and then quickly disconnected a few wires. 'That should do it!' he grinned. Now, let's get *out* of here.'

They dashed across the yard, climbed over the high fence and ran for their lives – the two boys helping Madulo, who was struggling. They ran until they couldn't see the warehouse building any more. Then they ran a little further just to make sure they had gone far enough. They sank down in the thin shade of a thorn tree to try to get their breath back.

Noah was the first to recover. 'We can't hang around here,' he said in a worried voice. 'We need to get as far away from the Boss as possible. We need to get to a police station!'

'Yeah, but how?' Letso asked in a tired voice. 'I think I've had enough of this adventure. And Madulo is just about finished. We should get her home as soon as we can.'

It was Madulo who spotted the little cloud of dust first. And as she watched it, the dust cloud turned into a donkey cart with a little grey donkey and a little brown donkey. Driving the cart was an old man. And sitting beside the old man was . . . was . . . the naughty boy from the bus! She was sure of it. The nearer the cart came, the more sure she was.

Madulo stood up, shading her eyes against the low, late afternoon sun. 'Hello!' she shouted. 'Hello! You're the boy I saw on the bus from Gaborone! Remember me?'

Lema tried to pull her cousin down, to stop her shouting. 'They might be dangerous!' she said. But Madulo was grinning from ear to ear. 'No! That boy's not dangerous. They *will* help us.'

As the oldest (and tallest), Noah felt he should be the one to address the old man.

'Rra! Rra! We need your help!' Noah called out.

'Hee banna!' exclaimed the farmer, stopping the donkey cart with a soft call to his donkeys. He was surprised to see the children appearing so suddenly out of nowhere. 'What are you doing here?'

'Rra, we will explain if you just help us get back to the village,' said Noah. 'We need to get to the police station.'

'Why do you need a police station? What have you children done? Where did you come from?'

It was all getting too complicated. Madulo stepped forward. She spoke to the old man, but she looked at the boy. He would understand. She knew he would understand.

'We . . . well, we found the thieves who have been stealing school computers from the government. They took us prisoner . . . but we managed to escape . . . but now we are in danger until we get to the police and get them to arrest the thieves.'

The old man seemed to find this difficult to take in all at once. He took his hat off and scratched his head for a minute.

'Well . . . I'm going the other way . . .' he said slowly. 'I've *been* past the police station, and now I am going to my cattle. My grandson here,' he turned and smiled at the boy from the bus, 'who is here for the school holidays, is going to learn what a cattle post is all about.'

'But . . . but we have to get to the police station. These men could kill us if we don't get away!'

'Ijo!' said the farmer, not really believing the story.

'Please Rra, please get us to the police station,' pleaded Madulo.

The boy interrupted, still watching Madulo. Maybe he thought she would tell his grandfather about his trick on the bus? Madulo said nothing. She had thought it was a clever trick. And the bus driver and conductor were *not* nice men!

The boy seemed to make up his mind suddenly. 'Grandfather . . . I know this girl. She was on the bus . . . the bus I took to my aunt's house before she brought me here. I think we can trust her.' He looked at Madulo – hard – to see if he could. She smiled back at him.

The old man made up his mind. He started to turn his donkeys and his donkey cart. 'Come on then. But I don't want any trouble from any of you, do you understand?'

The four children scrambled into the donkey cart. The boy from the bus gave Madulo a shy smile. 'Thanks, hey,' he said softly.

'Thank *you*,' Madulo whispered back. 'We needed your help!'

The police station fence was high, with spikes at the top, to stop people jumping in and out. The walls were painted blue, with a white stripe that ran across all the buildings.

Sergeant Dipalo was a tall tough-looking man with wide eyes. The farmer and the children walked into his office together and began their story.

'We just wanted to puncture their bicycle tyres because they had ruined our football,' explained Letso.

'But the men turned out to be thieves! They steal computers,' offered Lema.

'And Madulo hit a rock and hurt her wrist and scraped her knees,' Letso added, wanting to be in the conversation. 'But that didn't stop them tying her up and hurting her.'

'And both the thieves are called Manny,' Madulo put in, 'so we call them the Mannys.'

The policeman was looking a bit confused, but he knew the old man. If the children were with him, they could be trusted, he thought.

'And where are these computers?' he asked, trying to keep up.

'In a warehouse in the industrial estate, past Newtown,' answered Noah. 'We can take you there.' He was almost jumping up and down with worry. 'If we wait too long . . . they could escape!'

Sergeant Dipalo was not going to be hurried. He turned respectfully to the old man.

'And you Rra? Are all of these your grandchildren?' Sergeant Dipalo asked.

'No Sergeant!' he answered, standing at attention and sounding very much like a soldier in a drill, 'Just the one. I only brought the others here, Sergeant!'

Sergeant Dipalo considered everything. It was true that there was an alert out about the missing computers. Maybe he should . . .

'Please!' Madulo said desperately, with her most winning smile. '*Please*!'

The sergeant, who had been having a quiet time – up to then – gave a big sigh. This was going to be complicated.

'Come then, take me to this warehouse,' said

the sergeant, picking up his official hat. 'Let's find out what this is all about.'

Madulo, Lema and Letso climbed into the back of a police pick-up truck, the kind that has bars on the windows. Noah was allowed to ride in the front with the sergeant and another policeman.

'Wait!' Madulo called from the back. 'What about the boy from the bus? He ought to come too. He helped us when we needed help most!'

Sergeant Dipalo rolled his eyes. 'OK, OK,' he said. 'We might as well have the whole lot of you!'

The farmer left in his donkey cart, quite pleased that he had played his part in the order of justice – and sure that his grandson would turn up at the cattle-post when he was done. He was the kind of boy who always came home at the end of the day.

★★★

The Mannys were not having a good day. In fact, they were having a *really* bad day. Probably the worst day they had ever had. Not only was the Boss angry with them for bringing those troublesome kids back with them. He was also angry with them for losing the computers and messing up his careful plans. Now they were locked up as well – and the only way out was through a window that only a kid could get through! And worst of all, the kids had disappeared! Things were looking very bleak, very bleak indeed.

And that was *before* the Boss came looking for them. The Boss was not having a good day either – and it had just got a whole lot worse. First he had wasted quite a lot of time shouting for the Mannys to come and load some computers. Then he had wasted more time looking everywhere for them. He had finally found them, locked in the store and yelling for help – with no key anywhere in evidence. Then he had to waste more time getting the door open. This wasn't easy; it was a strong door. And when he finally finished wasting all that time, it was only to find that those kids had escaped.

'Boss, heh . . . heh . . . heh . . . they are just children. What can they do?' offered Manny

One nervously; knowing very well that what had happened was going to get him and his friend into serious trouble.

'Just *children*? Just *children*?' screamed the Boss. 'If those children heard or saw something they were not supposed to, they could ruin me. And if they ruin me . . .' he whispered, inching closer to the two Mannys, 'GUESS WHAT HAPPENS TO YOU!'

The Boss pushed past the two Mannys and ran out of the warehouse towards his brand new Mercedes Benz. He screeched out of the grounds without saying a word to the two Mannys. He wasn't about to take chances, so he left them to deal with the consequences. He had to make himself disappear!

The two Mannys looked at one another, wondering what to do. There was really only one thing to do. They had to get away too. They jumped into their old truck. Manny One tried to start the engine, but nothing happened when he turned the key.

Klavvvrr-vr-vrr-vrrvrr . . .

He turned the key again, closed his eyes, said

a silent prayer, and pumped the accelerator pedal repeatedly, as hard as he could.

Klavvvrr-vr-vrr-vrrvrrr . . .

'Come on . . . come on . . .' he coaxed.

But the truck was not about to go anywhere.

The two Mannys had no idea about trucks and they had no time to figure anything out either. And so they set off on foot. They left the warehouse with all its contents – and the dead truck in its spot.

They decided that their best chance was to cut across the big Newtown grasslands into the next village, Salabjwe. Manny One had a cousin there who would surely take them in. No one would think to look for them in Salabjwe, so they could hide out there for a while.

Chapter Four

The big grey police pick-up came tearing down the dusty road, guided by Noah. They finally arrived at the warehouse, where the children were ordered to stay in the pick-up while the policemen went inside the warehouse to investigate. After a few minutes, when nothing dangerous seemed to be happening, they went after him anyway.

'Whoo, whoo, whoooo . . .' whistled Sergeant Dipalo, when he saw the scale of the operation. 'This is serious!'

He immediately telephoned his supervisor on his mobile phone. He was going to need back up – lots of back up!

'This is Sergeant Dipalo calling . . . Yes, Superintendent Moloko. Of course Superintendent Moloko. I understand, Superintendent Moloko . . . but . . . yes, Superintendent Moloko . . . we have found a warehouse full of boxes and boxes of what we believe to be stolen goods. It's mostly computers and other home electronic equipment. They are still in their original packaging with labels that say where the shipments were supposed to go.'

There was a silence while Superintendent Moloko had a chance to say something again, and then the good sergeant went on, 'It appears the thieves were here not long ago. There is a truck in the yard that the children claim was used by two of the suspects. We believe they might still be nearby, so we'll start a search straight away.'

Madulo and the others had given Sergeant Dipalo a clear description of what the two Mannys looked like. And he was confident that, once they were in his custody, the two Mannys would tell him what he needed to know about their boss. Sergeant Dipalo was well pleased. This would look good on his service report. He might even get a medal!

'Er, Sergeant?' It was that boy, the boy on the donkey cart again.

'Yes?'

'Well, I just wanted to suggest that . . . if I was running away from the police . . . I would maybe go to one of the smaller villages. Maybe they are local men. They will need help to get away, now that their truck is here.'

'Exactly right,' Sergeant Dipalo said – having thought about it for a second. 'Exactly what I was thinking! Er... which village were you thinking they might head for?'

'Well... if I were running away from the police, I'd go to the nearest one. That's what I'd do.'

'Exactly what I was just going to say myself,' Sergeant Dipalo agreed. 'Now let's get over there and make an arrest!'

★★★

The two Mannys walked as far as they could go. Unfortunately, that was not very far, as Manny One was as big as an ox and weighed more than a ton of bricks. Manny Two was not used to having any kind of exercise – at all – and that made it very difficult for him to get himself cross-country to the next village.

Suddenly, they heard a siren – a police siren. And it was coming from somewhere very close!

When they stopped to look around, they saw a great big cloud of dust storming up behind them, and before they knew it, the police – in the form of Sergeant Dipalo and five children – had clamped down on them.

'Stop. You! Stop right there!' shouted Sergeant Dipalo. ' St-o-o-o-op!'

The Mannys knew it was over. Nothing they could do now would save them. In a way, it would be a relief to be safely behind bars, where the Boss couldn't get at them. Both Mannys automatically put their hands up above their heads and gave themselves in.

It was Sergeant Dipalo's big moment. 'Do you both answer to the name Manny?' Neither of the Mannys said anything.

Lema jumped in. 'Yes they do. And they stole those computers, then kidnapped us and nearly killed us!'

'Stay in the truck young girl, and be very quiet,' replied Sergeant Dipalo, quite annoyed by the interruption. This was *his* big moment.

'What are your real names?' asked Sergeant Dipalo.

Still nothing.

'Fine, we will do this at the police station,' he sighed. 'Come on then, in you go.' The Mannys crawled right to the back of the truck where they were as far away as possible from those dreadful *children*. Once they were all huddled up in the back of the pick-up, Lema could not stay quiet any longer. 'You see? You see what happens to bad thieving men? Now you are going to be locked up in jail for ever and your children will never see you again.'

'Shut up Lema!' scolded Letso and Madulo. For someone who scared very easily, Lema sure did stir things up.

Back at the police station, the two Mannys were led into a small square room with no windows. The children were – very firmly – left outside. The questioning process started with Superintendent Moloko making a very graceful and dignified entry, his uniform pressed to a creaseless finish and his shoes perfectly shined.

'So, what do we have here?' he asked.

The two Mannys looked sorrowful as they wondered what their fate would be.

'The first thing you have to do is tell me all about your operation. But before that, I want to know your real names, where you live and what you do for a living?' said Superintendent Moloko. 'You first,' he said, pointing at Manny One.

Manny One looked as if all the air had been sucked out of him.

'Em . . . em . . . my name is Kabo Sabatho. I live in Serowe. I-I-I don't have a job, Sir.'

'And you?' the superintendent went on, pointing to the other Manny. 'What's your real name?'

Manny Two looked at his shoes. 'My name is Petros Moilwa. I live in Serowe. I don't have a job either.'

'Is that so?' scowled Superintendent Moloko. 'Now, you tell me what I need to know. Actually, on second thoughts, tell me why you are both called Manny?'

The two Mannys looked at each other. 'The Boss said it was easier. Everybody in our operation is called Manny. Except him. He's called the Boss.'

'Hmm. I see,' said Superintendent Moloko, who didn't really understand.

'Now . . . tell me everything!'

The two Mannys looked at one another, trying to decide who would speak first. After a long pause, Manny Two began telling all.

'We were hired by a man we call the Boss. His . . . his . . . his real name is David Setima. He has a shop in the centre of Serowe called Riverside General Dealer. He has also built a large syndicate of people who work for him in and around Serowe. He hired us to collect merchandise off a goods train in the village, and take it back to the warehouse.' Manny Two looked up at the ceiling, as if to pray to God to forgive his sins.

'The Station Master also works for the Boss, you see,' continued Manny One. 'His job is to off-load the goods from the train.'

'This man,' said Superintendent Moloko, 'this "Boss" man, where is he now?'

'We don't know,' replied Manny Two. 'He took off.'

'Without us,' added Manny One, looking helpless.

'In his brand new Mercedes,' Manny Two added helpfully. 'It is a maroon Mercedes Benz E2OO, with the licence plate B 123 BGY.'

'Hmmm, I see,' said Superintendent Moloko thoughtfully. 'Sergeant Dipalo?'

Sergeant Dipalo sprang to attention. '*Sir*!'

'Go and arrest the Station Master at once. And put out a call to all stations to look out for this Mercedes.'

Then his eye fell on the children, who were still waiting outside the interrogation room. 'And sergeant . . .'

'*Sir*!'

'Send those children home!'

★★★

After they pleaded with and begged him, Sergeant Dipalo agreed to let the children watch the exciting arrest of the troublesome Station Master.

Sergeant Dipalo didn't want to alarm the Station Master, so he sent one of his men to ask for information about train times. While he was talking to the Station Master, Sergeant Dipalo walked into the office and locked the door.

'Heeey, what the . . . ?' the Station Master started to ask.

'Sir, are you the Station Master here?'

'Well, yes, you know I am!'

'And what is your name, Sir?'

'Er . . . Sam Selepeng,' he blinked quickly and then his eyes darted from left to right, like a rabbit caught in headlights.

'Mr Selepeng, you are under arrest. Please come with us,' said Sergeant Dipalo.

The Station Master turned around and tried to jump out of the big steel window. But this was not his lucky day. His body was only half way through the window when Sergeant Dipalo caught him by his legs.

'Ooohh no,' said Sergeant Dipalo, 'let's rather use the door. Come on.'

Superintendent Moloko was pleased with Sergeant Dipalo's work for the day. He put Sam Selepeng in the jail cell next to the two Mannys.

It wasn't as simple to find the Boss. But the police locked up his shop and stopped all business. They sent a message to all the police across the Central and Northern Districts, to arrest a man of his description, driving a maroon Mercedes Benz E2OO, bearing the licence plate number B 123 BGY. Sooner or later, someone would catch him. Superintendent Moloko was sure of it.

Chapter Five

As he drove along at top speed, the Boss thought about how he would cross the border into Zimbabwe, where his friends would help him go into hiding. He had abandoned his flashy car and drove a smaller Volkswagen with a different number plate.

But the police in the northern city of Francistown were on the alert and were ready for him. They had roadblocks all along the highway, and stopped each car that went by for a thorough search. Unfortunately for the Boss, they had his photograph too, so when they stopped him, they recognised him immediately.

He was arrested and locked up in a jail cell at Francistown central station, ready to be taken back to Serowe the next day.

Madulo, Noah, Lema and Letso were driven back to Nkuku's home. They were exhausted after their amazing adventure, one they could never have imagined. Nkuku and Maemo were very surprised to see the children arriving home in a police car. Tea was immediately offered, as is the custom in Botswana, and accepted by a thirsty Sergeant Dipalo, who was only too happy to tell his important side of the story.

Just then, the news came on the national radio.

'With the help of four courageous children, the police in central Serowe have uncovered a crime syndicate that stole goods from the village railway station. These goods, mainly computers, radios and other electronic equipment were bound for schools and hardware shops in the region . . .'

Nkuku looked at the children proudly. But they could see in her eyes that she was going to have something to say to them later about having gone off on their own in the first place.

It was a good start to the holiday, Madulo felt, even if it was going to be a few days before she could do handstands again. And there was a bit more excitement when they were called in to the police station to be presented with certificates of bravery and had their hands shaken by the most

senior police officer in Serowe. Then there was the excitement of seeing their pictures in the newspapers. and then Madulo's mother was on the telephone wanting to hear everything that had happened.

So the rest of the holiday passed really, really quickly. It seemed like no time before Madulo was back at the bus station in Gaborone, jumping off the bus and into her mother's arms.

Her mother was excited to hear all about Serowe and everything that had happened there, but all Madulo had to say was, 'Mama, I'm hungry. What's for lunch? I hope you've cooked my favourite dish.'

And that was really the end of Madulo's very serious adventure.